GRAND OLD LADIES

North Carolina Architecture
During the Victorian Era

JoAnn Sieburg-Baker, Head Photographer
Sterling Boyd, Author of Introduction
Marguerite Schumann, Editor

The East Woods Press
Charlotte, North Carolina
New York   Boston

Front Jacket — The romantic Queen Anne-style dwelling, Victoria, at 1600 The Plaza in Charlotte, one of the first houses of its time to be listed on the National Register of Historic Places, has been painstakingly restored by its owners William and Frances Gay. The house displays high-quality workmanship throughout. It contains skillfully crafted hardware, elaborate gas and electric chandeliers, colorful art glass windows, ceramic tiles, multicolored stenciling, and varying woods (cedar, walnut, pine, oak, American chestnut, and two types of cherry). While Victoria was being built early in the Gay Nineties, newspapers had almost daily accounts of the "stylish house taking shape on Tryon Street." When, in 1915, the house was moved to its present location, the original cast-iron picket fence went along. (Color photograph by JoAnn Sieburg-Baker.)

Back Jacket — The entry to the Jacob Lott Ludlow House in Winston-Salem. An exterior photograph of the house is shown in figure 85. (Color photograph by JoAnn Sieburg-Baker).

Library of Congress Cataloging in Publication Data

Schumann, Marguerite E.
   Grand old ladies.

1. Architecture, Victorian—North Carolina.
2. Architecture—North Carolina. I. Title.
NA730.N8S38 1984   720'.9756   84-48035
ISBN 0-88742-013-3

Typography by Raven Type
Printed in the United States of America

An East Woods Press Book
Fast & McMillan Publishers, Inc.
429 East Boulevard
Charlotte, N.C. 28203

GRAND OLD LADIES

North Carolina Architecture
During the Victorian Era

For Tom Lambeth

A Victorian gentleman
cast in twentieth-century mold

Third Street Houses, Wilmington

Acknowledgments

While the majority of the pictures in this book are those of JoAnn Sieburg-Baker, head photographer, it was necessary to add the work of a number of others to achieve a balance in subject material. Special thanks must go to Randall Page for Figures 7, 11, 24, 26, 27, 28, 29, 30, 35, 66, 68, 78, 99, 103, 114, 121, 126, 139 and 143. Also included, many from the staff of Archives and History in Raleigh, are Catherine Bishir, 49, 79, 140, 141; Dick Blount, 70, 81; Mary Jo Brezny, 137, 138; Hugh Brinton, 123; Charles Clark, 44, 89, 117; Diane Davis, 9; Ben Floyd, 130; Mary Ann Lee, 43, 69; Ruth Little-Stokes, 124, 125; Clay Nolen, 115, 128; Neil Pearson, 39, 40, 64; Steven Schwartz, 41, 97; Michael Southern, 31, 38, 45, 46, 50, 55, 142; Gwynne Taylor, 19; Ed Turborg, 82; and Tony Wrenn, 34. The Charlotte Mecklenburg Historic Proper-ties Commission contributed Figures 91, 112 (Dan L. Morrill), 75 and 133 (Thomas W. Hanchett). Other photos came from the Biltmore Estate, 118, 119, 120; State Capitol Photo, 3; Travel and Tourism, 1, 83, 84; and these units of the University of North Carolina at Chapel Hill: the News Bureau, 4; the Photographic Laboratory, 5; and the North Carolina Collection of Louis Round Wilson Library, 6.

Most of these additional photos were chosen from the negative collection in the State Library, where Dick Langford cooperated with unfailing good humor. For four months, Daphne O'Brien worked on this project in those files — not merely flipping through photos, but the infinitely harder task of "reading" negatives — in her search for specially assigned subjects. A particular word of praise is due to her and her careful record-keeping, as she discovered for herself the joys of research among North Carolina materials.

A number of persons gave special expert help: Davyd Foard Hood of Raleigh, Peter Kaplan of Raleigh, Ron Holland of Asheville, Tom Hanchett and Dan Morrill of Charlotte, and these who opened doors for the photographer — Watson Brown of Tarboro, Dr. Douglas Kelling of Concord, Jerry Lundy of Statesville, Laura Phillips of Winston-Salem, Evelyn Sowers of Salisbury, and James Robert Warren of Wilmington.

Grateful acknowledgement is made to the following for permission to reprint fragments from the writings of North Carolina authors that serve as captions for some of the pictures:

To Da Capo Press, for the quotation from Broadus Mitchell; to Doubleday and Company, for O. Henry; to Houghton Mifflin, for Charles Chesnutt; to the North Carolina Department of Cultural Resources, Division of Archives and History, for David Stick; to Travel-Holiday (Travel Building, Floral Park, N.Y.) for writing by Jonathan Daniels and Ovid Williams Pierce originally appearing in *Holiday* magazine; and to the University of North Carolina Press, for passages of Zoe Kincaid Brockman, Hope Summerell Chamberlain, John Harden, Bernice Kelly Harris, Harriet L. Herring, Robert B. House, Sydney Nathans, and Bill Nye.

Further thanks is given to these individuals: Richard Goldhurst for the writing of Harry Golden; Kennette M. Hall, for the work of Lewis Philip Hall, and to Mrs. Guy Owen and Mrs. Thad Stem, Jr., for the writing of their respective husbands. These authors gave permission personally, and they are a special group of friendly folks — Daphne Athas, Doris Betts, Frances Gray Patton, Reynolds Price, Anne Russell, Max Steele, and Mena Webb.

Foreword

"Where are all the historic houses — and the silos?" I mourned when I moved to Durham in the late 1960s after four decades in Wisconsin, America's dairyland and the paper manufacturing capital of the nation.

To my Midwestern eyes, a historic house was a Victorian house, bristling with ornamentation, ennobled by a romantic tower, and surrounded by a dignified wrought-iron fence. This was the sort of house — grandly historic — built by paper manufacturers in the prosperous valley with which I was familiar. The same men built their paper mills along the Fox River to designs that owed much to Italian palaces.

I quickly discovered a comforting silo in Durham, on a golf course. But it took me longer to find a historic house as I defined it, for the city had lost many of its 19th-century treasures when a freeway had been cut through the center of town, near the mills where tobacco tycoons chose to live to admire daily the work of their hands. That freeway was my introduction to the idea that economic progress often meant destruction of the architectural symbols of the past.

Happily, I soon began to discover other kinds of historic houses, in this state two centuries older than the state I had known. But the longing for a good bristling Italianate or mansard-roofed Victorian structure was largely unsatisfied until I joined the North Carolina Chapter of the Victorian Society in America. The systematic travels of this group around the state, visiting some of North Carolina's most charming small towns that are frequently off the beaten tourist path, taught me a great deal about the last century's ideas of beauty, and the way prosperity and self-respect were expressed in home and workplace. It also demonstrated to me that there were bonds still shared between northern and southern culture during a period when divisiveness was very fresh in the nation.

In addition to the ongoing education I received in Victoriana, the local chapter of the Victorian group supported the grant application to the Z. Smith Reynolds Foundation, whose generous gift made this book possible. The Victorian Society, however, is in no way responsible for inadequacies in this work; they are my fault.

As the group of collected photos grew, I became aware that the same quality revealed in the pictures was sometimes revealed in the writings of North Carolina authors as they recalled the scenes of their youth. Therefore I searched dozens of books for literary fragments that seemed to fit the Victorian milieu, in order to use them as photo captions.

When the time came to fit photos and captions together, I had to take some liberties. I had intended, for instance, to use writing by Doris Betts to illustrate house pictures in her hometown of Statesville, but the photos I had in hand didn't exactly fit. She had written to me, "The sources of these fictions are real — specific houses on Walnut Street and Davie Avenue in Statesville, in which I planned to live when grown up and rich, writing novels in those tower bedrooms." I apologize to Professor Betts that her words had to be placed elsewhere geographically. But then, she has not written her novels in a tower bedroom, but in the good lands of Lee and Chatham Counties! A charming paragraph by Max Steele, too, describing summertime life on a porch, had to be measled with dots to eliminate a boxwood-bordered path that did not fit the photo. These good people will understand that nature does not always imitate art.

There were many splendid Victorian buildings in the state whose photos had to be dropped because there were too many modern intrusions nearby or because a noble subject was photographed under adverse lighting conditions. For this, I am sorry.

I hope that *Grand Old Ladies* will encourage North Carolinians to look at the built world around them with new eyes. Beyond that, I hope it will stimulate some to acknowledge and respect the remnants of Victoriana that remain. I hope, too, that it will encourage many to join the small army of little old ladies in tennis shoes (of which I am a proud member), as well as their more numerous, more chic, and much younger companions in preserving what is left of a period that has much more to recommend it than simple nostalgia.

Marguerite Schumann

Introduction

The Victorian Age was rich in energy, imagination, and creativity. The Princess Victoria ascended the throne of England in 1837 and reigned as Queen until her death in 1901. This remarkable woman was immortalized by having her name given to one of the most ingenious and expansive periods in modern history. Striking developments in the arts went hand-in-hand with important developments in industrialization and social awareness. Victoria's reign began with the intense excitement of the European romantic movement — with paintings by Turner and Delacroix and compositions by Chopin and Mendelssohn. It ended with the masterpieces of Monet and Cezanne in art and of Debussy and Mahler in music.

The "Victorian Age" in America occurred between the end of Andrew Jackson's presidency in 1837 and the beginning of Theodore Roosevelt's in 1901. The years between these two dates saw rapid westward expansion, the development of women's rights, the abolition of slavery, the presidency of Abraham Lincoln, the Civil War, the growth of railroads, commerce, industry, and labor unions, anti-trust and interstate commerce legislation, the Spanish-American War, and, as one might expect, periods of economic inflation and depression.

In the arts and literature, Americans in the early years of Victoria's reign admired the landscape paintings of Thomas Cole and the scenes of everyday life painted by George Caleb Bingham. They read the writings of James Fenimore Cooper, Edgar Allan Poe, and Henry David Thoreau, and they listened to the music of Stephen Foster and Louis Gottschalk. The social and political disruptions caused by the Civil War in the middle of the century were followed in

the later years by a wealth of artistic
creativity. The writings of Mark Twain,
Walt Whitman, and Emily Dickinson,
the paintings of Thomas Eakins,
Winslow Homer, and Mary Cassatt, and
the music of Edward MacDowell, Scott
Joplin, and Charles Ives represented
high points in late Victorian America, as
did major developments in the growth of
cities, in industry, and in social evolu-
tion. A burgeoning middle class provided
more and more clients for architects and
builders, who modified their work according to the needs of a changing
culture.

If we consider the Victorian Age as in-
cluding the entire sixty-four years of
Victoria's reign, we are able to see the
great sweep of thought and creativity
which ranged from the romantic movement of the 1830s, with its love of imagination and sentiment, its fascination
with the past and the unusual, and its
belief in freedom and individualism, to
the dawn of the 20th century. This book
surveys Victorian architecture in North
Carolina as that architecture reflects the
richness of the Victorian Age. We see the
attitudes and ideals of the Early Victorian period (1837 to the 1850s), the Mid-
Victorian period (the 1860s and 1870s),
and the Late Victorian period (the 1880s
to 1901).

American architecture from 1837 to
1901 ranged from the imaginative and
inventive romantic designs of the Early
Victorian period through the increas-
ingly practical and materialistic designs
of the Mid-Victorian period to the more
expansive and organized designs of the
Late Victorian period. The age began
with the Greek Revival and ended with
the early works of Frank Lloyd Wright.

During this era Americans looked to
the architectural ideas of England and
France for inspiration. England was the

Zebulon Latimer House, Wilmington

main source for most of the styles found here, but the French had a strong influence later in the century.

Beginning in 1837 and continuing through the 1840s and 1850s, the two most important architectural styles in America were the Greek Revival and Gothic Revival. The widely ranging imagination of romanticism expressed in these Greek and Gothic styles was cut short by the Civil War.

The Greek Revival style had been established in England when Victoria became Queen in 1837, and its popularity lasted through the 1840s. The style had the same duration in America, though in some regions of the country — particularly the South — the Greek style lasted well into the 1850s. This interest in ancient Greece was part of a fascination with the classical world which had begun in Europe in the 18th century and which produced the neo-classical style in art and architecture of the late 18th and early 19th centuries. During these centuries both Greece and Rome played large roles in the intellectual life of Europe and America. The interest in Rome and the revival of Roman architecture preceded the Greek Revival, with Thomas Jefferson's architectural designs being prime examples of this classical revival style. By the 1820s, however, the interest in Greece was increasing, and by the 1830s the Greek Revival style had become more important than the Roman.

The most handsome example of Greek Revival architecture in North Carolina was the State Capitol in Raleigh (fig. 1). Dedicated in 1840, the building symbolized American fascination with the Greek ideals of political democracy and individual freedom. Designed in a bold masculine style by the firm of Town and Davis of New York, the strongly propor

tioned portico with its Doric columns brought to mind then, as it does today, the great buildings of classical Athens — especially the Parthenon. In the interior of the Capitol the architects used Ionic columns with their graceful forms and proportions, as seen in the Legislative Chamber (fig. 2). The illusion of space found in this room was created by combining a large domed ceiling with four huge wall piers. While the Greeks did not use domes, the Romans did, and architects in the early 19th century did not hesitate to mix styles and sources if they thought the building would benefit from the mixture. Town and Davis combined Greek columns with Roman domes to produce a classical room with a maximum amount of open, usable space.

The Old State Library in the Capitol (fig. 3) provided a striking contrast to the rest of the building by its medieval or Gothic Revival style. The library was distinguished by its slender coupled columns supporting low pointed arches. This type of arch was called a Tudor arch from the style of architecture which existed in England during the reign of the Tudor kings Henry VII and Henry VIII. The presence of both the Greek and the Gothic styles in the Capitol may seem surprising, but combining Greek with Gothic was a typically romantic and Victorian practice. By the 1830s, when the Capitol was being designed, the revival of Gothic architecture had begun in England and the style was gradually appearing in America. The Greek Revival exterior of the Capitol, with its Doric columns and pilasters, provided the dignified neo-classical quality of an important public building. The interior, with its Greek columns, refined ornamental details, and Roman dome, provided an impressive setting for contemporary politics. The Gothic style of the library recalled the libraries of the great medieval monasteries and universities, suggesting the scholarly function of that room.

In 19th-century England the rise of nationalism helped popularize the Gothic Revival as a style because of the great heritage of English medieval architecture. In America, however, the Gothic Revival was popular because it was new, and contrasted markedly with the Greek style. The romantic mind, intrigued by the religious fervor of the Middle Ages, would ultimately relate the Gothic Revival to the religious revivals and interest in nature of the early 19th century.

The Capitol's library was a significant example of the use of the medieval style by one of the most important architectural firms in America, that of Ithiel Town and Alexander Jackson Davis. Through personal and professional contacts North Carolinians consistently selected firms of both national and regional importance, while also employing local designers, builders, and craftsmen.

The Playmakers Theater in Chapel Hill (fig. 4), designed by Alexander Jackson Davis, was completed in 1851. The building resembled a Greek temple with its rectangular plan and imposing portico. On the front, four columns supported a triangular pediment. At a glance, the capitals of the columns appeared to be Corinthian, with leaves derived from the acanthus, a type of fern. On closer look, we see that Davis used the tobacco leaf along with wheat and corn to symbolize North Carolina's major agricultural products. The building was originally conceived to house both a library and a ballroom.

In the 1840s and 1850s handsome examples of the Greek Revival style were constructed throughout the state. New West Building in Chapel Hill (fig. 5) was completed in 1859 by the English architect William Percival. Massive Doric pilasters adorned the front of the building. New West originally housed a dormitory and a literary society, literary and debating societies being extremely popular at this time. A rare photograph shows the Dialectic Literary Society Hall in New West as it appeared in about 1900 (fig. 6).

The main building of Peace College in Raleigh (fig. 7) was also completed in 1859, on the eve of the Civil War. It was constructed of brick, a less expensive and more generally used material than the granite of the Capitol in Raleigh. The great Doric columns were also of brick, covered with stucco and painted white to resemble the marble originally used by the Greeks. Town and Davis always used a correct classical column, one that tapered gradually from bottom to top, then curved slightly to give the column a less static look. This method was called "entasis." Because the columns of Peace College are straight, we must assume that the builder was not as familiar as Town and Davis with this difficult technique.

A spectacular example of the Greek style was the City Hall and Thalian Hall in Wilmington (fig. 8), with its monumental portico supported by Corinthian columns. Designed by James Montague Trimble of New York and completed in 1858, the building was unusual in several ways. First, it was intended to house two totally different civic functions — a city hall and a theater. This attempt to contain two major functions in one building was motivated by practical, utilitarian concerns of the mid-19th century. The planning of buildings to house large and complex institutions and services was one of the major contributions of Victorian architecture, reaching its greatest development in the Late Victorian period.

The second unusual feature of this building was the blending of Greek and non-Greek elements in the exterior design. In other Greek Revival buildings seen thus far, windows were rectangular with flat tops, or lintels, and flat horizontal moldings above them. A more ornate type of window became popular in the 1850s. It was derived from a style of medieval architecture, the Romanesque, which predated the Gothic. The windows in Thalian Hall, topped by round arches and curved moldings, were based on Italian Romanesque designs.

The City Hall stood as an outstanding example of Greek Revival architecture, as well as an excellent illustration of the blending of styles and periods which had become so prevalent in the mid-century. This borrowing from different sources and mixing of various styles is called "eclectic," and it well represents the vast range and imagination of the Victorian mind.

The tempo of change increased in the 19th century as popular taste moved rapidly from one style to another. The 19th-century mind, energetic in one way, restless in another, constantly moved from country to country and from age to age in its search for ideas and expressions.

The Greek Revival style, while perfect for large imposing public buildings, was, curiously enough, equally suitable for churches and private dwellings. The Christian Science Society Church in Goldsboro (fig. 9) was built as a Presbyterian Church in the 1850s. The eloquently simple front with its sunken porch, columns, and pilasters produced the effect of a Greek temple. The bold tower rising above the pediment was probably intended to support a lofty spire. The tower, in having three pilasters across the front for decoration, was unusual because the general rule of classical design was to have an even, not an odd, number of columns or pilasters. The architect of this church ignored the rules to create what he considered to be a proper design.

St. Paul's Church in Randleman (fig. 10) was an extremely simple version of a Greek Revival church, having a completely plain front crowned with a pediment supporting an impressive tower. Even without columns or pilasters, the Greek style of the building was evident from the proportions of the design. The width of the building was equal to its height as measured from the top of the foundation to the top of the pediment. The triangular pediment was one-third of the total height of the front. These strong, equal proportions, divided into thirds, were the standard formula for Greek composition. The solid proportions identify the Greek style of the church.

Domestic architecture in the Greek Revival style varied a great deal. There were elegant houses with small porticos, such as Eaton Place in Warrenton (fig. 12). Connemara, Carl Sandburg's home in Henderson, built in 1838 (fig. 11), was notable for its large, one-story portico with full pediment. A massive, two-story portico characterized the Edward Belo House in Winston-Salem (fig. 19).

Eaton Place, the Nathaniel Green House (fig. 12), and the Somerville-Graham House (fig. 16) were designed in the 1840s by the architect Jacob Holt. Located in Warrenton, all had large balanced facades and small elegant porches with Doric columns of wood. The plans of the houses were completely symmetrical, having central hallways flanked by rooms on both sides. In Eaton Place, the large curving fanlights over the entrance door and the second floor window were not Greek revival in origin, but came from the earlier Federal period of about 1800. In the Greek Revival period the windows, or "lights," over the doors were completely rectangular with flat tops, as in the Somerville-Graham House (fig. 16).

The graceful staircase of Eaton Place (fig. 13) with its curving handrail and simple baluster supports also originated in the Federal period. For this house the architect combined the graceful Federal forms of curving fanlights and stairs with the more powerful, angular forms of Greek architecture. For the interior of the Green House (fig. 15), Holt used rectilinear wooden door frames, a hallmark of the Greek style. They had wide molded panels and square corner blocks with central circular ornaments.

For the Somerville-Graham House (figs. 16 and 17) Holt designed perfectly proportioned Doric columns for the porch and doorway, with simple Greek key moldings above the columns and across the tops of the windows (the diamond panes were added after 1900). In the interior (fig. 18) he used a classic Greek Revival mantelpiece — paired Doric columns supporting a heavy flat lintel, or frieze, with a projecting cornice forming the shelf. The walls of Greek Revival houses were usually plaster, either painted or wallpapered.

The great portico of the Edward Belo House in Winston-Salem, of about 1850 (fig. 19), was magnificent. The capitals of the Corinthian columns were cast-iron, not wood, and painted white to resemble wood or marble. By this time wooden capitals were too expensive to make by hand and remained susceptible to weather damage. Cast-iron was cheaper to produce and impervious to weather. This use of metal represented Victorian practicality and the steady advance of industrial technology.

Wrought iron was a beautiful hand-crafted art of the early 19th century, as seen in the Oakdale Cemetery gate in Wilmington (fig. 20), but it was eventually replaced by cast-iron, which was quicker and less expensive to manufacture. The use of cast iron for structural and ornamental purposes increased greatly in the 1850s and continued through the 1860s and 1870s. It was so successful, in fact, that cast-iron work was often added to earlier houses to update them or replace perishable wooden columns. For example, the Dr. Josephus Hall House in Salisbury (fig. 21) was built in 1820, but its porch was added in the mid-century.

The Barracks in Tarboro, designed by William Percival in the 1850s (fig. 22), demonstrated the increasing ornateness of the Greek Revival style. Using only two Aeolic columns to support the portico, the architect included windows with both flat and arched tops and added elaborate brackets in pairs to support the cornice. An ornamental cupola on the roof served as a light source for the stairhall below. The very elaborate exterior of this house made an interesting contrast with the elegant simplicity of its interior (fig. 23).

Without doubt, the most elaborate example of the Greek Revival house was found in the Bellamy Mansion in Wilmington (fig. 24). Completed in 1859 for Dr. John D. Bellamy, a physician who was also a director of the Bank of Cape Fear and a director of the Wilmington and Weldon Railroad, the house was probably designed by Rufus Bunnell, a New England architect. It was modified and built by a Wilmington architect, James F. Post. Post had moved to Wilmington from New Jersey about 1840, and was professionally active in the city throughout the mid-century.

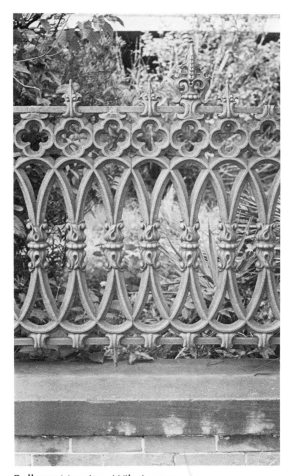

Bellamy Mansion, Wilmington

A delightful small version of the Greek style was found in the Waldo-Darden Hotel located in Hamilton (Martin County) (fig. 25). A long, narrow building with an imposing portico, it today seems almost overbalanced by its imposing front. Because it was not wide enough to have a central hall with flanking rooms, the designer placed the hallway on one side so that the rooms to the left could be as large as possible. The Ionic columns, which were probably designed by a local architect-builder, were too wide and too short in their proportions, and the capitals' curving volutes were too large for the size of the columns. Though not perfectly correct in their design, the columns were wonderful in their vigor, and the entire portico exuded a gusto and a drama which far outshown the size of the building.

In terms of creative energy, the Garland Buford House in Caswell County (fig. 26) was one of the most spirited examples of the Greek style in the state. The carved wooden brackets of the cornice gave an animated energy to the house which was matched by the fancy woodwork of the porch. The sober rectangular piers used in place of columns were all but lost in the wealth of added decoration. By 1850 ornamental brackets and fancy work were no longer tediously carved by hand, for the mechanical saw had been invented and all types of ornamental woodwork could be produced rapidly and relatively inexpensively. The love of variety and detail on the part of the owner could easily be satisfied by the imagination of the craftsmen.

The interior woodwork (fig. 27) was fantastic in its totally non-Greek character, particularly when compared to the

Greek houses by Jacob Holt in Warrenton. The Garland Buford House woodwork, full of multiple curves, was entirely the creation of a local craftsman — in this case, probably Thomas Day, a highly respected free black man who was an important designer and producer of furniture and woodwork in the 1840s and 1850s. Houses such as this one, with vivid evidence of work done by regional artisans, are sometimes described as being in a "vernacular" style.

Cooleemee, in Davie County (fig. 28), presented a stunning and inventive plan for the hot Southern climate. The arrangement of the house was an "X", with wings opening off a central stairhall which rose the full height of the house and was lighted by a cupola on the roof. Each room had maximum ventilation from large windows and interior doors opening into the light-filled central hall. The plan of the house was originally published in 1847 by W. H. Ranlett in his book, *The Architect*. The house had a sophisticated design which maximized the latest word in convenience and comfort. Though it retained the traditional Greek style, it also suggested some of the newer ideas of the 1850s. The elegant Ionic columns and the pediments on each wing represented the Greek style, while the windows, with round tops and double arched panes, repeated the Italian Romanesque style found in the City Hall in Wilmington.

The interior of Cooleemee was stunning (figs. 29 and 30), from the curving staircase with its solid handrail and ornamental balusters to the magnificent Ionic columns in each of the main rooms. All of the exterior columns and interior woodwork were made in Philadelphia and shipped by water to Fayetteville, North Carolina, where they were taken by ox cart to the house site in Davie County.

Houses in the Early Victorian period varied from the more rigid, rectangular plans of Greek style houses to the flexible plan of Cooleemee. An innovation similar to Cooleemee's, but more curious, was introduced in the 1850s by Orson Fowler, an American health addict. He proposed an octagonal plan for houses, believing it offered increased air circulation for personal health, along with maximum space utilization and minimum expense. The Inkwell House, near Amity in Hyde County (fig. 31), represented a small version of this unique idea.

By the 1850s the Greek Revival style had just about run its course, and other styles were coming into fashion. There were three styles which became popular at this time: the Italian Villa, the Italian Renaissance, and the Oriental, Moorish, or Persian style.

The Italian Villa style was created in England shortly after 1800 by the architect John Nash, and became popular in America in the 1840s and 1850s. This type of house allowed for a more flexible interior plan while creating a picturesque exterior that blended more naturally into the landscape. John Nash's original design borrowed a tall tower with round-topped doors and windows from medieval Italian Romanesque architecture; porches, or "loggias", with columns, arches, and large overhanging cornices with brackets from Italian Renaissance architecture; and triangular pediments from Roman architecture. Completely eclectic in style, the finished product was, indeed, picturesque. The fluid lines, freer plan, and essentially non-classical composition were very different from the more formal Greek style. One of the most outstanding examples of this style in America was Blandwood, the house of Governor John M. Morehead in Greensboro (fig. 32), which was designed by Alexander Jackson Davis in the mid 1840s.

By the 1850s houses such as Coolmore in Tarboro (fig. 33), represented modified versions of the Italian Villa style, without the tower but with round arched windows, suggestions of pediments, and large overhanging eaves with elaborately designed brackets. The taste for increased ornamentation in the 1850s was evident in this house, from the fancy cupola to the brackets, windows, and doors.

The Caswell County Courthouse (figs. 34 and 35), built between 1858 and 1861, was designed by William Percival. Its powerful cornice was derived from Italian Renaissance architecture. From Italian Romanesque architecture came the ornamental brickwork, with its small arches at the tops of the walls, and the windows. The great swelling curve in the center of the facade was undoubtedly a sample of Percival's creative dexterity. The cast-iron railing, the round arches, the unique Greek-type columns, and the elaborate ceiling of the courtroom are perfectly preserved today. This type of building, with its many design elements taken from Italian architecture of different periods, was sometimes referred to as being in the Italianate style, or the Bracketed style because of the overhanging eaves and heavy brackets.

The second architectural style to become fashionable in the 1850s was the Italian Renaissance, which, although similar to the Italianate, was different in that almost all of its design elements were based exclusively on Italian Renaissance architecture. The style originated in England in the 1840s in works by Sir Charles Barry. The impressive Zebulon Latimer House in Wilmington (fig. 36) was built in this style in 1852 by James F. Post. The great cubic mass of the house, its powerful cornice, frieze, and brackets, and the bold quoins at its corners were all derived from Italian Renaissance palaces in Florence and Rome. To these Renaissance forms the eclectic American architect added ornate pediments above the windows, a porch with handsome Greek Aeolic columns, and a side porch with cast-iron filigree. Many of these decorations on the exterior of the house were pre-fabricated: the capitals of the columns and the pediments over the windows were made of metal, and the brackets were made of an artificial stone compound formed in molds. The cast-iron fountain stands in its original location at the corner of the house.

In the interior of the Latimer House (fig. 37) the decorative woodwork around the doors and windows followed the basic forms of the Greek Revival. The white marble mantelpiece with its arched opening and carved details was not Greek, however, but the latest word in new 1850s fashion. Mantelpieces such as this were either imported directly from Italy or produced in a city like New York and shipped throughout the country. The sliding doors between the parlors were devised earlier in the century to provide a more flexible living arrangement. The doors could be closed, thus separating the two rooms into smaller spaces, or could be opened to produce one large space.

This Renaissance style was also employed successfully for the later Griffin and Martin Law Office in Williamston (fig. 38). This small building was graced with an elegant arcade, or loggia, comprised of three arched openings surmounted by a handsome cornice with frieze and brackets.

The third architectural style which came into fashion just before the Civil War was the Oriental, Moorish, or Persian style. All three of the names related to the same exotic style. The Temple of Israel, in Wilmington (fig. 39), was a perfect example of this late romantic design. The domes on the towers and the horseshoe-shaped arches above the windows and entrance door gave the building its Oriental character. The interior (fig. 40), however, was more medieval than Oriental. The capitals of the ornamental columns, with their tightly curling leaves, came from European architecture of the Romanesque and early Gothic periods. (Even Oriental exoticism needed something extra in this age of high eclecticism.) The Temple of Israel, the first synagogue in North Carolina, was built for the first Jewish congregation in the state. Its date, 1875, was late for this style, but its lateness may be attributed to several factors: the founding date of the congregation, the social upheaval caused by the Civil War, and the economic depression which followed it.

Turning now to another important style of the Early Victorian period, we find the Gothic Revival as second in popularity only to the Greek. The Gothic style was particularly popular for churches, educational institutions, and houses. Religious revivals in England in the early 19th century produced for both Catholics and Protestants an interest in medieval architecture as a style which would represent the newly felt emotions and attitudes of the age. The Gothic style was also adopted for colleges and universities because it recalled the emphasis on scholarship found in the great medieval universities. Hence we find the Gothic library in the Capitol in Raleigh.

The Gothic Revival style was widely received in North Carolina. St. James Episcopal Church in Wilmington (fig. 41) was built in 1838 by Thomas U. Walter, an important architect from Philadelphia. Walter was known primarily as a Greek Revival architect, but he and contemporaries such as Town and Davis worked in both Greek and Gothic styles. St. James was a superb model of this romantic style. Constructed of brick, its walls were covered with stucco and painted a deep buff color to imitate the original stonework of medieval architecture. The great tower, with its long pointed-arch windows and tall pinnacles, formed the focal point of the design and emphasized the asymmetrical plan of the building. Medieval architecture was not as rigidly balanced as the Greek, which contributed to its popularity in the 19th century. The long nave with crossarms, or transepts, formed a Latin cross plan. Walter ornamented the exterior with arched windows lightened by decorative tracery, steeply angled gables, salient buttresses against the walls, battlements at the edge of the roof, and a tall tower with even taller pinnacles. This 19th century design reflected the great upward thrust of medieval cathedrals and parish churches. In the interior (fig. 42), the wooden structural system supporting the roof was left exposed, as it had been in medieval architecture. Decorative details such as trefoils and quatrefoils were added, thus enhancing the Gothic quality.

For Christ Church (Episcopal) in Raleigh, designed in the mid 1840s and completed in 1854 by Richard Upjohn of New York (figs. 43 and 44), the architect emphasized the non-symmetrical plan of the building by moving the tower away from the main part. The church had rough granite exterior walls, while the interior followed the Gothic tradition of revealing the magnificent wooden structural system of arches, posts, and beams which supported the roof.

Smaller versions of churches in the Gothic style were built throughout the state, many of which were constructed of wood, a simpler and less expensive material than brick or stone. With any architectural style there is usually a specific time period when the style is particularly popular, even though examples of that style can be built long after the major period has ended. This was the case with two wonderful smaller churches, the United Methodist Church in Fairfield (figs. 45 and 46), built in 1877, and the St. Barnabas Episcopal Church in Snow Hill (figs. 47 and 48), built in 1893. Both edifices were distinctly Gothic, but had subtly different personalities. The small mission church of St. Barnabas seems quietly spiritual, while the United Methodist Church has a decidedly noble air.

For domestic architecture, the Gothic Revival style produced two basic forms: the Castle and the Pointed Cottage. Behind the Castle style was the English love for houses reminiscent of medieval castles, stimulated in the early 1800s by the novels of Sir Walter Scott.

Following this Castle style was the Commandant's House in Hillsborough (fig. 49), part of the Military Academy and built in 1860. It was described at the time as being either in the Castle-lated or Scottish Baronial style. The second form of Gothic house was the Pointed Cottage. It was generally built of wood, although many examples such as the Capehart House (fig. 50), were constructed in brick and stone.

The Capehart House in Kittrell was built from about 1865 to 1870. It was a typical Gothic cottage marked by an asymmetrical plan, a steep roof with projecting gables, lacy ornamental wood-

work along the eaves, and windows with pointed arches and diamond-shaped panes of glass. The lacework, commonly called "gingerbread," only remotely resembled actual Gothic ornament. Very important in this type of wooden house, yet something which is often overlooked, is the actual structure of the building. On the exterior, the siding was nailed on vertically, with a narrow "batten" that protected the edge of adjoining boards. This Board and Batten exterior protected an inner structure composed of light-weight vertical studs set at regular intervals along the wall — exactly the same system used today in both wooden and brick veneered buildings. The use of lightweight wooden studs replaced 18th- and early 19th-century heavy timber construction. This lighter weight construction evolved into what was called the "balloon frame." It was developed in the Midwest in the 1850s as a practical answer to the need for mass-produced, rapidly built, low-cost housing. It became widely used throughout the country in the mid-century, and was made possible by the mass production of prefabricated parts by newly developed machines.

The particular Gothic style represented by the Capehart House was called by different names: it could be either a Gothic Villa or Cottage, depending on its size; a cottage in the Pointed Style, referring to the use of pointed-arch windows and steep gables; a Board and Batten cottage, referring to its construction; or a Downing cottage, referring to the name of the man who popularized it. Andrew Jackson Downing, of New York, advocated this style of house in his books on architecture which appeared in the late 1840s and early 1850s. Downing described the practical character of these houses, emphasizing their freer plans and more functional room arrangement. He also pointed out the generally lower costs of these houses, especially the smaller ones designed for the working man. And finally, in keeping with the avid interest in nature in the early 19th century, Downing believed that this type of house fitted more intimately into the surrounding landscape than did the imposing Greek style houses. Downing was extremely interested in gardening and landscaping, and preferred an informal garden setting for his houses. This interest in harmonizing architecture with nature came when American landscape paintings were greatly admired, and when cities such as New York were bursting at the seams with expansion. Anticipating the future growth of New York and the resulting destruction of the open land around it, Downing suggested that the area which is now Central Park be preserved to insure that the natural landscape could be enjoyed by later generations. This project was completed later in the century by Frederick Law Olmsted, the great landscape architect who designed the gardens and grounds at Biltmore House in Asheville.

Houses such as the Dr. A. B. Nobles and Cheshire-Nash Houses in Tarboro (figs. 51 and 52), and the William Fields House in Greensboro (fig. 53) illustrated the widespread popularity of Downing's ideas, as well as the love of North Carolinians for the decorative beauty of the Gothic style. Patterned roofs, porches, gables, gingerbread, and arched windows all joined together to bring the Middle Ages to the mid-19th century. Some of the most enchanting examples of these Gothic houses were the smallest ones, such as the Matthewson House in Tarboro (fig. 54). A simple cottage adorned with a wonderful porch of lacy Tudor arches and lattice supports, this house was typical of those built from the 1840s to the 1880s. Simple and comfortable, the house was one manifestation of the creative range of Victorian design. The pavilion in the cemetery at Fairfield (fig. 55) was a further example of the simple charm of Early Victorian Gothic.

Tarboro's much larger Pippin House (figs. 56 and 57) illustrated a style created in the 1850s which survived the Civil War and continued with some variation into the later part of the century. The sharp triangular gables and round windows with tracery were derived from the Gothic, but the simple brackets, or "modillions," under the eaves, and the rectangular posts of the porches, were Greek in origin. A hybrid mixture of Greek and Gothic, the house perfectly illustrated the creative freedom enjoyed by Victorian architects and their clients in the mid century.

The Mid-Victorian period in America was marred by the Civil War, but emerged vigorous and volatile. Prior to the war, the national debt stood at $67 million. After the war, in 1866, the debt was about $2.5 billion. The presidency of Ulysses S. Grant (1869 to 1877) suffered from social and economic instability. A major financial panic shook the nation in 1873, caused by "inflated currency, unlimited credit, reckless speculation, and over-expansion." For the South, the war years and the following Era of Reconstruction (beginning in 1867 and lasting into the 1870s) were particularly difficult — physically, economically, and psychologically. Life did go on, however, and new architectural styles appeared which reflected the increasing prosperity of the nation. Adaptations of the Italianate and Gothic styles continued to be constructed, but there emerged one new style in particular which epitomized Mid-Victorian America — the Mansard style.

The Mansard style can be seen in the Cabarrus County Courthouse in Concord (fig. 58). It was completed in 1876 to designs by G. S. H. Appelget. The great double-hipped roof with its steeply sloping sides and the dramatic curving roof of the tower represented the most fashionable architectural style of the time. The Mansard style originated in France in the 1860s, influenced by the major additions being made to the Louvre Palace by the Emperor Napoleon III during what is known in French political history as the Second Empire. In America, the style had various names, all meaning the same thing: the Mansard style, referring to the name of the 17th century French baroque architect, Francois Mansard, who popularized this type of dramatic hipped roof; the Second Empire style, referring to the time in French history in which it was being revived; and the Franco-American style, referring to the style's origin in France and popularity in America.

For North Carolina, the Cabarrus County Courthouse was particularly interesting, for it combined pre- and post-Civil War designs. The tall round-topped arches set into the walls, the rounded windows, and the pediment in the center of the facade were from the Italianate style of the 1850s. The steeply sloping hipped roof and elaborately framed dormer windows were purely Mansard, as was the robust convex curve of the tower roof. The design of the building combined both past and present, ignoring the disastrous war in between, and looked towards the future.

A simplified version of the Mansard style was Faith Hall (fig. 59), part of Barber-Scotia College, founded in Concord in 1867. Established as a Presbyterian seminary for black women, it was one of the first institutions dedicated to "training leaders for educational and social service."

As prosperity developed in the 1870s, houses in the new style arose throughout the state. The Mansard style was rich in ornamentation and bold in dimension. It suited well this period of a return to material well-being and physical comfort. Though it lacked the classic vigor of the Greek style, and the high whimsy of the Gothic or Italianate, it did bring to post-war North Carolina a sense of stability. Raleigh's Dodd-Hinsdale House, of 1879 (fig. 60), with its elaborately designed tower, was a perfect example of the effect of affluence on the culture. The Redmond-Shackleford House in Tarboro (fig. 61) was a particularly handsome Mansard house, complete to the cast-iron cresting on the roof. The interior of this house (figs. 62 and 63) had a spectacular decor, with stenciled patterns on walls and ceilings echoing the rich surfaces and curvilinear elements of the exterior.

The Banker's House in Shelby (fig. 64) combined Italian Villa elements of the 1850s with the new style, while the Concord house of John Milton Odell, the great textile mill manager and owner, was a perfect example of the French style (fig. 65). One of the most striking examples of the Mansard style was the Saluda Cottages at Flat Rock (fig. 66). A house was built on this site in the 1830s, but the magnificent Second Empire structure which stands there today certainly dates from the 1870s. The designers used mirrors to increase dramatically the size of the main staircase, while a smaller, more practical cast-iron staircase displayed rich baroque curves (figs. 67 and 68).

Houses of all sizes were built in the new style, and were appointed with wonderful curving roofs and verandas.

The Heck House in Raleigh of the early 1870s (fig. 69) and the Mansard Roof House in Fayetteville of the early 1880s (fig. 70) were relatively small for their time, but the second story rooms under the high curved roofs contained large amounts of very usable space. Even though the Fayetteville house was built in the early 1880s, the Mansard style had already gone out of fashion after the 1870s. With the beginning of the Late Victorian period, innovations were coming into being which expressed the ideals and attitudes of the later years of the century.

Most of the major styles of the Late Victorian period were based on European Romanesque and Gothic architecture. Minor styles were based on French Renaissance architecture and on 18th-century European and American architecture, but, in general, the Middle Ages dominated Late Victorian design. Some of the medieval designs were similar to ones found in the Early Victorian period, but their forms were usually quite different. Late Victorian public buildings and churches were more massive and powerful than those of the earlier period. Private homes retained their flexibility and convenience, but lost the romantic whimsy of the earlier examples. The buildings could still be very ornate but the most progressive ones exhibited a tighter unity in their plans and a greater organization in their overall effect.

Some of the most dynamic designs of the later 19th century were created by the Boston architect Henry Hobson Richardson. Based on French and English Romanesque architecture, his ideas influenced architects throughout the country who worked in the Richardson Romanesque style of the 1880s and 1890s. Richardson created important designs in the 1870s but his influence on his contemporaries was greatest in the Late Victorian period.

One of the most attractive Richardson Romanesque buildings in the state was the Statesville City Hall (fig. 71), originally built as a Post Office and Federal Building in 1892 by Willoughby J. Edbrook, an architect from Washington, D.C. The round arches over the doors and windows were similar to ones found in the Italian Villa and Bracketed styles, but their forms were heavier and more powerful. The walls appeared to be much thicker and the broad horizontal lines of the composition were strongly accentuated. The brick and stone used in buildings such as this one were usually of a deep reddish brown. Decorative accents were then added in lighter colors. The overall effect was one of a powerful mass with a horizontal emphasis, rich in color and texture, placed firmly on the ground.

An additional important effect of a Richardson design was the strong handcrafted quality — the sense of a work created by human hands rather than by machines. Richardson and other architects of his time reacted against the exuberant industrialization of this era. One of the reasons they so admired medieval architecture was because of the quality craftsmanship that distinguished it. They feared industrialization because it threatened to turn laborers and craftsmen into urban factory workers.

One of the most important influences on the late 19th century's appreciation of medieval architecture in both England and America were the ideas and writing of the English architectural critic John Ruskin. His two major books, *The Seven Lamps of Architecture* and *Stones of Venice*, presented his views on the importance of medieval architecture. He appreciated the depth of religious feeling in medieval architecture. He also admired the visual beauty of the buildings themselves, the varying colors and textures of their stone work, the sense of integrity in their use of real materials rather than imitations, and the personal involvement of their craftsmen in hand-cutting stones and ornament. All of these ideas were in total contrast to the industrialization of mid-19th-century England and to the increasing use of pre-fabricated metal in architectural design.

Many of Ruskin's ideas were similar to those of Richardson. Richardson, though, preferred Romanesque architecture, while Ruskin preferred Gothic. Ruskin was also immersed in the visual and emotional aspects of architecture while Richardson was interested in the functional qualities of his designs. The emphasis on functionalism and practicality of the earlier Victorian periods found a worthy successor in Henry Hobson Richardson.

Architects in North Carolina approached the Romanesque style in diverse ways. Edbrook's City Hall in Statesville was "pure" Richardson. The designer of the Julius I. Foust Building at the University of North Carolina at Greensboro (fig. 72), one of the two original buildings of the school, created a more ornamental version of the style in 1892 using contrasting colors in the stonework. Richard Morris Hunt, a New York architect who, like Richardson, had studied at the Ecole des Beaux-Arts in Paris, designed All Souls' Episcopal Church in Asheville (fig. 73) in the 1890s. The church had a strong and simple Romanesque quality with a few Gothic pointed-arch windows thrown in for effect. The bold geometry, unadorned surfaces and ground-hugging ef-

fect set this building apart. It was a far cry from his work at Biltmore House, but, like other Victorian architects, Hunt worked easily in various styles.

All that remains today of the First Presbyterian Church in Salisbury (fig. 74) is the great Romanesque tower. Designed in 1891 by Charles W. Bolton of Philadelphia, it stands today like a remnant from a fairy tale castle.

Buildings such as Biddle Hall of Johnson C. Smith University in Charlotte, built in 1884 (fig. 75), the New Hanover County Courthouse in Wilmington (fig. 76), and the North Carolina School for the Deaf in Morganton (fig. 77) represented extremely large-scale works in the Romanesque style and were also ultimate statements in Late Victorian institutional design. The Courthouse, built in 1892 by the Savannah architect A. S. Eichberg, provided complete facilities for the administrative offices of the county. The School for the Deaf, also built in 1892 by Adolphus Gustavus Bauer, a Philadelphia architect who moved to Raleigh, satisfied the complex requirements of this unique institution. What had begun in Wilmington's City Hall in the 1850s culminated in the School for the Deaf in the 1890s. The styles had changed from "Greek with a little Romanesque" to "Romanesque with a little Gothic," but the ideas were the same: to design a building to house one or more complex functions. The very existence of the School for the Deaf demonstrated Late Victorian social awareness and concern for the disabled. The great size of the building and its medieval accents did not conceal the overall sense of unity and functionalism in its design.

Belmont Abbey (fig. 78), built in the early 1890s, carried Gothic architecture from the Early to the Late Victorian

Solomon Weil House, Goldsboro

periods. Much larger than the earlier medieval style churches in the state, the Catholic Abbey admirably represented the continuing waves of Gothic influence which swept through American architecture in the 19th century. If the design of the church seemed to be more "real" or more "archaeological" than the earlier ones, it was because Late Victorian architects were more careful to model their designs on specific buildings. The two great towers of the Abbey were polygonal spires of unequal height. In medieval Europe the different heights would have resulted either from the length of time involved in building the church, or from the varying financial problems encountered during its construction, or from damage to one of the towers by lightning or fire — as was the case with Chartres Cathedral in France.

The architect for the United Method-

ist Church in Oxford (fig. 79) took the idea of two unequal towers and ran with it, the result being a highly picturesque design of the Late Victorian period. Solid walls, pointed arches, and one great tower were freely and creatively combined to produce a sturdy Protestant house of worship.

Small churches such as the chapel of St. Augustine's College in Raleigh (fig. 80) followed the simpler ideas of Richardson and Hunt. Designed by a clergyman, Lemuel T. Delaney, and built in 1895 by the students of the College, the chapel's medieval style was indicated by a few Gothic arches, while the long low silhouette related the building to its site and emphasized the natural materials of its construction.

St. Joseph's Episcopal Church in Fayetteville (figs. 81 and 82) was chartered in 1873 by black members of St. John's Episcopal Church. The present building was constructed in 1896. Supposedly based on a church in England, St. Joseph's followed closely the horizontality and large undecorated roof areas of Richardson's style. The wooden shingles used on the exterior wall represented the Shingle style and were derived from Richardson's and other architects' use of natural textured materials in their work. The interior of the church underscored this naturalism with wall and ceiling surfaces of wood. Jewel-like windows created by Tiffany and Company of New York beautifully expressed the principle of using natural forms in art.

In domestic architecture of the 1880s and 1890s, styles were based in varying degrees on medieval sources. The Executive Mansion (governor's home) in Raleigh (fig. 83) was one of the most outstanding houses of its day. It was begun in 1883 to the designs of a noted Philadelphia architect, Samuel Sloane, and was completed in the 1890s. Sloane was aided during the design and construction by Gustavus Adolphus Bauer, the Philadelphian responsible for a large number of buildings in the state.

In the arrangement of the Mansion, Sloane devised a building which was well-designed for a hot climate. Large windows, porches, balconies, wide hallways, and rooms with high ceilings satisfied functional and personal needs. The three large gables on the exterior were derived from medieval architecture and were also reminiscent of the pronounced gables found in the Swiss Chalet style. In the Philadelphia Centennial Exposition of 1876 the Swiss exhibition included a complete chalet that enchanted visitors and architects alike. Elements in the Executive Mansion suggested a relationship to Swiss forms, as well as to the ideas of the contemporary

English architect Charles Eastlake. A follower of Ruskin, Eastlake liked the concepts found in medieval architecture and suggested using properly controlled machinery to produce attractive ornaments. The columns of the Executive Mansion, with their alternating wide and narrow sections, were based on Eastlake's designs. They were turned on a mechanical lathe. This bold and chunky wooden column was characteristic of the Eastlake style. The warm tones of red brick, brown wood and buff stone used on the exterior of the Mansion and in the patterns of the roof indicated the desire of the architect for a naturalism that was in the Ruskin-Richardson medieval tradition. The elements of color and texture, and the relaxed flow of the building's side porches reflected Sloane's naturalist ideals.

The interior of the Executive Mansion (fig. 84) epitomized Late Victorian eclecticism. The entrance hall displayed classical columns while the principal rooms had plaster decorations based on 18th-century rococo and neo-classical forms. The impressive but unassuming exterior masked an interior of neo-classical elegance.

Eastlake style houses appeared in abundance in the 1880s and 1890s. Their wooden exteriors with clapboards, shingles, spreading verandas, and turned columns represented the comfort and prosperity of the middle classes in this period of economic growth. The Col. Jacob Lott Ludlow House in Winston-Salem (fig. 85) and the Royster-Bryan House in Tarboro (fig. 87) were excellent examples of Eastlake houses. Their interiors were similar in their use of deep-toned woodwork with simple, rectilinear forms. The Ludlow House (figs. 85 and 86 and back jacket) retained, curiously enough, the Greek Revival style of window and door frames. The dining room of this house was particularly wonderful because it was furnished and wall-papered in the style of William Morris, another Englishman who, following Ruskin, detested industrial fabrication and loved the warm visual beauty of medieval design. The deep-toned interior of the Royster-Bryan House (fig, 88) radiated warmth, serenity, and contentment. Because of the slender porch columns and the delicate wooden open-work decorations of these two houses, they are often described as being in the Stick style, another variant on medieval wooden houses. The imposing Hawkins-Hartness House in Raleigh (fig. 89) and the more unassuming Mott-Simmons House in Statesville (fig. 90) represented variations on the Swiss Chalet and the Eastlake styles. As seen in these examples, the great eclecticism of the 1850s was easily matched by that of the 1880s and 1890s. Both houses had a unique type of roof — a clipped gable which was known as a "jerkin head" roof. This type of roof came from the Swiss Chalet. The porches and columns of the Hawkins-Hartness House resembled those of the Executive Mansion, while those of the Mott-Simmons House came straight from the earlier Italianate style. The Mallonee-Jones House in Charlotte was a further example of modified Eastlake design (fig. 91), while the Liddell-McNinch House combined Eastlake and Shingle elements for a unique effect (fig. 92). Medieval, Swiss, and Eastlake were all variants on Gothic architecture as seen and created by the Victorian eye and mind.

Korner's Folly, in Kernersville (figs. 93 and 94), stood out as an absolute extravagance among the fairly restrained medieval designs of the 1880s. Its romanticism was a complete anachronism in the later years of the century. The folly was the unique creation of a unique mind, that of owner and designer, Jules Korner, who also popularized Bull Durham tobacco. Korner took a Gothic cottage in the Pointed style and blew it up to gigantic dimensions. Spectacular Gothic gables projected upward like witches' hats. Brackets, railings, balconies, chimneys, and a castellated wall were combined to produce a medieval confection. Yet, the inside was resplendently baroque and rococo.

As variations on medieval themes carried American architecture towards the end of the century, one particular new style appeared which enlarged, and confused, Late Victorian design — the Queen Anne style. The house named Victoria, built in 1891 in Charlotte (cover photograph and figs. 95 and 96), was a classic example of this style. The central gable, the circular tower placed at the front corner, and the spreading porches were hallmarks of a style which began in England in the 1860s and was in full force in America by the 1880s. This style went through more transformations than any other of the Late Victorian period. It began as a revival of architecture of the Queen Anne period in England, of about 1700. For Americans Queen Anne would be associated with houses built in or near Williamsburg, Virginia, in the early 1700s, such as Westover on the James River. These houses were essentially classical in their design, with rectangular plans, red brick walls, and high hipped roofs. Roman columns or pilasters and pediments were used as decorations around the front doors. To this basic scheme English designers, such as Norman Shaw, added a circular tower modeled from the French Renaissance, a style being revived at this time in France. From this point on, the Queen Anne style was metamorphosed until it appeared in the Victoria House with a full complement of clapboards, shingles, and verandas in a quasi-Eastlake style. The interior of the house (fig. 96) had simple doorframes similar to those found in the Eastlake style, and lacy ornamental panels. The panels were restrained — their compositions followed basic geometric shapes of squares, circles, and triangles filled with flower patterns, starbursts, lattice work, diaper patterns, or spindles with round balls. The look was ornamental, but not excessive. These designs had none of the exuberance of those of the 1840s and 1850s. Interiors ornamented with cedar, walnut, pine, oak, and cherry beautifully manifested the Victorian's love for natural woods.

As the late 19th century progressed, the Queen Anne and Eastlake styles were often combined, with the result that it became difficult to tell which style a building was intended to represent. With a little effort, patience, and luck, an analysis can be made. The key to Queen Anne design is the use of a tower, in numberless variations; the key to Eastlake style is the use of vigorous turned columns.

Larger and more expensive examples of the Queen Anne style were found in the Blades House in New Bern (fig. 97) and in the Charles T. Holt House in Alamance County (fig. 99). These houses represented the maximum elaboration of the style. In the interiors (fig. 98), elements of 18th century design appeared in the dark, varnished wood dadoes along the lower parts of the walls and in pilasters, friezes, and cornices around windows. The comfortable and sociable lifestyle of the age was given full evidence in the large verandas (fig. 100) and spacious gardens with gazebos (fig. 101).

The variations of Queen Anne themes were limitless, as exemplified by Raleigh's Capehart House (fig. 102), Oak Ridge's Oakhurst (fig. 103), Salisbury's Gaskill-Pierce and L. H. Clement houses (figs. 104 and 105), Concord's James Dayvault and William G. Means houses (figs. 106 and 107), Statesville's W. A. Thomas and C. M. Steele houses (figs. 108 and 109), and Charlotte's Overcash House (fig. 110). In the Gaskill-Pierce House, the tower itself was eliminated, but a suggestion of it can be found in the circular pavilion at the corner of the porch.

The Daniel Branson Coltrane House in Concord (fig. 111) eliminated the tower completely and emphasized classical cornices and slender Roman columns similar to those found in American Federal architecture of about 1800. This house was on the verge of moving out of the Queen Anne style into a new style, the Colonial Revival. In the Blades and Holt houses (figs. 97-99) and in the J. P. Carr House in Charlotte (fig. 112), the columns used were not in the Eastlake style, but were modifications of classical Roman columns. The Blades House also had interior woodwork in an 18th century style. These houses represented the gradual transition from the Queen Anne and Eastlake styles to the Colonial Revival. The Colonial Revival was developed in the East in the 1890s by the New York architectural firm of McKim, Mead, and White, and culminated in the early 20th century.

Two buildings in North Carolina suggested an early beginning of the Colonial Revival: the Chatham County Courthouse in Pittsboro (fig. 113) built in 1881 by Thomas Womack, and the Broughton Hospital (fig. 114) in Morganton (originally the Western North Carolina Insane Asylum), completed by Samuel Sloane and A. G. Bauer in the 1880s. The Courthouse was in the Classical Revival style of the early 19th century and the Hospital was in the Georgian style of mid 18th-century America.

The Philadelphia Centennial in 1876 helped stimulate a new interest in things American, which resulted in a new American architectural style, the Colonial Revival. Technically speaking, the colonial period in America had ended in the early 1780s with the end of the American Revolution. But as the Colonial Revival blossomed in the early 20th century, it contained everything from 17th-century America to the Greek Revival of the 19th century.

In the late years of the 19th century, some houses were designed with a minimum of ornamentation, for reasons either of taste or economics, most probably the latter. The Thomas Wolfe Memorial in Asheville (fig. 115) was a large but sober house for the time, standing outside the mainstream of ornamental design of the period.

The Rumbough House in Asheville (fig. 116), now the Highland Hospital, was built in 1892, and provided a striking contrast to other houses of its day. The simplicity of its long horizontal lines, broad roofs, and minimally ornamented surfaces gave this house a power not found in any of the Queen Anne or Eastlake houses. Suggestive of the strong designs of Richardson, this house stood at the crossroads of the 19th and 20th centuries. Paralleling designs by the English architect Charles Voysey in the early 1880s and by the American Frank Lloyd Wright in the late 1890s, the Rumbough House was a prelude to the 20th century.

Biltmore House in Asheville was a masterpiece of Victorian eclecticism (fig. 117). Begun in 1890 and completed in 1895, the house was built by Richard Morris Hunt for George W. Vanderbilt. Hunt had studied in Paris at the Ecole des Beaux Arts and knew by heart the French Renaissance and baroque styles taught there. He also had a very refined eye for detail and a well-defined sense of composition. The design of the house was based on the chateaux built in the Loire River Valley in France by King Francis I in the early 16th century. This French Renaissance style was a blend of both French Gothic and Italian Renaissance architecture. From the French Gothic came enormously tall steep roofs and elaborate ornamental details. From the Italian Renaissance came symmetrical plans and classical decorations. For the design of Biltmore, Hunt borrowed details from specific buildings in the Loire Valley: the great staircase to the left of the main entrance, with its parallel ramps running upwards in diagonal lines, was taken from the Chateau of Blois; to the left of the staircase the ground level arcade, the elaborately decorated windows, and the enormously tall roof of the main house were taken from the Chateau of Chenonceaux. These chateaux were two of the most popular of the Loire Valley.

The interior of Biltmore represented in the grand style the magnificence of Victorian design. The splendid staircase (fig. 118) had its origins in 17th and 18th century designs; the spectacular library (fig. 119) was based on Renaissance and baroque designs; and the stunning Palm Court (fig. 120) was distinctly Gothic. The general term for the style of Biltmore was either the Chateau style, referring to its derivation from French Renaissance chateaux, or the Beaux Arts style, referring to the 19th century French architectural school which popularized this type of revivalistic design.

The Victorian love of nature was illustrated at Biltmore House in the strikingly elegant Palm Court, which was actually a greenhouse included as part of the main house. The glass roof of the Palm Court was supported by metal beams designed and painted to look like medieval stone and wood. On a larger scale, the 19th century's fascination with nature was beautifully represented in the magnificent gardens and grounds designed by Frederick Law Olmsted. A pure 19th-century creation, and a monument to the imagination and creativity of both owner and architect, Biltmore House also symbolized the vast wealth created by industry and commerce that had accumulated in private hands by the end of the century.

While houses, public buildings, and churches provided ample evidence of the march of architectural ideas and styles through the Victorian Age, designs for industry and commerce demonstrated other aspects of Victorian creativity. This creativity was put to use, for example, in North Carolina's textile industry. During the period of economic growth that followed the Civil War, many large mills were built. The mill of the Columbia Manufacturing Company, at Ramseur on the Deep River (fig. 121), initially built in 1850, was enlarged in the 1870s. Industrial designs of this type reflected the logic, organization, and efficiency of Victorian labor methods. Southern textile mills were usually based on mills which had been constructed in New England earlier in the century, which, in turn, had been based on 19th-century industrial architecture in England. When ornamental details were used, they were generally in the Italianate style.

In conjunction with the textile mills, entire villages were built to house the employees. The concern of mill owners for the people working in the mills was part of an emerging paternal attitude toward the working man which developed in the Victorian Age. Two of the best-preserved mill villages in the state are Glencoe in Alamance County (figs. 122 and 123) and Coleridge in Randolph County. In these villages, the size of the homes varied according to the resident employee's work status, with the smallest going to a day laborer, the largest to a manager. Built primarily in the early 1880s, the wooden houses were designed for comfortable living. Decoration was minimalized, except for an occasional Queen Anne gable or a porch exhibiting the Italianate exuberance of a local craftsman (figs. 124 and 125). The dwellings were similar to 19th-century medieval-based designs and to simple American vernacular designs which could be traced back to the early 19th century, 18th century, and even to the 17th century. The villages also included general stores and churches.

The tobacco industry, like the textile industry, was built up in the post-war era. The Bull Durham Tobacco Factory in Durham (fig. 126) was constructed in 1875 as a grand version of an Italian Renaissance Palace. It originally housed the Blackwell Tobacco Company, the first large tobacco company in the state. The tobacco-curing warehouses of the Duke Tobacco Company were built in Durham in the late 1890s (fig. 127), following a type of Italianate design with ornamental brickwork. When studying the tobacco industry, it is interesting to note the Duke Homestead of 1852 (fig. 128), the home of Washington Duke, founder of the great company. Simple and sturdy, it followed a long tradition of practical American architectural design.

With the march of industry in the Late Victorian period came the growth of cities. To help meet North Carolina's urban growth, the Pomona Terra Cotta Manufacturing Company (fig. 129) constructed its factory to produce sewer pipes for cities throughout the state. These "bee-hive" kilns were the original kilns of the company. Zollicoffer's Law Office Building in Henderson (fig. 130), built in 1882, represented a type of small commercial building common in the 1840s and 1850s. The ornamented cornice and the porch, with its round and pointed arches, reflected the influence of Gothic and Italianate designs of the Early Victorian period. Progressive commercial projects of the mid-century utilized cast-iron for both structure and decorative purposes. The "iron-fronts," as they were called, were the forerunners of the 20th-century skyscraper. The Gidden's Jewelry Company in Greensboro (fig. 131) was begun in 1859 and enlarged in the 1870s. The Merchants and Farmers National Bank Building in Charlotte utilized the first locally made cast-iron from the Mecklenburg Iron Works in 1871 (fig. 133). The McMullen Building in Elizabeth City (fig. 134) was built in 1896. As the century progressed, pressed-tin became popular. For the McMullen Building, stronger cast-iron was used for the first floor while pressed-tin was used for the upper levels and cornice because it was lighter and less expensive. In 1896, the Fordham Drug Store in Greensboro (fig. 135) used pressed-tin for its ornamental

cornice and mortar and pestle. The interiors of the buildings (figs. 132 and 136) were neat and functional, with built-in cabinetry and decorative pressed-tin ceilings. They were narrow and long because street-front property was expensive. No wider than necessary, they ran the depth of the block behind the street. The enterprising William Waldrop built both his own house and the general store at Sandy Mush (fig. 137) in the mid-1890s. He was also the carpenter for Payne's Chapel (fig. 138).

Railroads developed rapidly after the Civil War. The passenger depot for the Seaboard-Coastline Railroad was built in 1900 in Hamlet (fig. 139) and is one of the few remaining Victorian depots. The presence of large flaring roofs followed earlier patterns by Richardson in the 1870s. The overhang protected passengers from the weather. Their simple wooden braces were derived from medieval architecture.

The Railroad House at Sanford (figs. 140 and 141) demonstrated the logic of the Victorian mind. Depots, as well as lighthouses, had their keepers, each of whom were housed right beside their respective places of work. The Sanford agent's house was an excellent representation of the Board and Batten or Downing design, even though it was built in 1872. By the 1870s the gingerbread of the Early Victorian period was out of fashion. In its place a more simple, practical type of ornamental brace was used in the tops of the gables. Of slender proportions, the braces, or "sticks," gave their name to the Stick Style, a variant of earlier wooden houses built in the medieval style.

As railroads expanded, so did travel, and it became much easier to go to such summer resorts as the Glendale Springs

Jeff White House, detail, Madison County

Hotel (fig. 142) or the Carolina Hotel in Pinehurst (fig. 143). The village of Pinehurst was created in 1895, with landscaping by Olmsted. Its first golf course was added in 1898, and in 1899 its hotel was built to provide additional accommodations for the highly popular resort.

The lighthouses of the Carolina coast, as sentinels of safety and symbols of protection, occupy a special place in the hearts and minds of North Carolinians. In the 1870s a major series of lighthouses was built along the coast. The Currituck Lighthouse (fig. 144) preserves the medieval style of its keeper's house of 1875. The Cape Hatteras Lighthouse of 1870 (fig. 145), the tallest lighthouse in America at 208 feet,

was constructed with a granite foundation and base, a brick shaft, and cast-iron brackets and railings supporting the beacon. The light originally burned oil. The Federal iron-clad gunboat, the *U.S.S. Monitor*, sank off the coast about fourteen miles from the lighthouse.

The rich visual detail in the homes, churches, and public buildings erected by North Carolinians in the Victorian Age reflected a highly sophisticated intellectual and aesthetic sensibility. Their explorations embraced both solemn purpose and individual impulse. The eye "secretly espying the world from behind lace curtains" must have been proud of the view, and encouraged by its promise.

Sterling Boyd

"The Victorian Age—
Rich in Energy,
Imagination
and
Creativity"

Fig. 1. State Capitol, Raleigh

But the oaks in the capitol square yet stood, and the
dignified little granite State House was impressive,
its deeply worn stone steps suggesting antiquity.
. . . The wide avenue that led to the left — there,
too, the old elms still stood. What a beautiful village
street it was, leading past the churches and the
deep-shaded girls' seminary with its ivy-covered
stone buildings, on by modest, shaded old homes
from whose yards the heavy odour of magnolias came!

> Walter Hines Page
> *The Southerner*

Fig. 2. State Capitol, Legislative Chamber, Raleigh

Fig. 3. State Capitol, Old State Library, Raleigh

Fig. 4. Playmakers Theater, University of North Carolina at Chapel Hill

It was an inspiration to see the president and the subordinate officers (of the literary society) seated behind mahogany desks on the rostrum with the society insignia on the background wall, facing a room full of members seated in a semi-circular arrangement of scroll-work iron chairs upholstered in red. The windows were draped in green velvet. And the present joined hands with the past in contemplation of the walls crowded with oil portraits of the great alumni of the Phi through the generations.

Robert B. House
The Light That Shines

Fig. 5. New West Building, University of North Carolina at Chapel Hill

Fig. 6. New West Building, Dialectic Literary Society Hall, c. 1900, University of North
Carolina at Chapel Hill

Fig. 7. Main Building, Peace College, Raleigh

Fig. 8. City Hall, Wilmington

Fig. 9. Christian Science Society Church, Goldsboro

Fig. 10.
St. Paul's Church, Randleman

Twilight Comes to Connemara
   (In Memory of Carl Sandburg)
Let the shadows stretch over Connemara
A goat cough in the rising fog;
Let a wind from the blue-gray Smokies
   stir hemlock and laurel
   under Big and Little Glassy
The Poet had said, "This is the place;
   we will look no further."

The singing Swede?
"He's long gone, oh, he's long gone"
and would have it no other way.

Set the green eyeshade by the Lincoln bust.
Let the guitar string go slack,
the Havanas lose their aroma. . . .

Let twilight come to Connemara.

Fig. 11. Connemara, Flat Rock

There are about ten steps leading up to the porch of the old plantation home and when I reached the top Mr. Sandburg was already outside to greet me. . . . I turned from him to take a long look at that breathtaking scene . . . and I greeted Sandburg with the first thought that came into my head: "Well I wonder what old Victor Berger would have said if he had seen this place." (Victor Berger, the first Socialist ever elected to Congress, was publisher of the Socialist paper *The Leader* on which Sandburg had worked in his early newspaper days.) Sandburg threw his head back and roared . . . but then he motioned me to a chair on the porch and began to apologize in all seriousness for a proletariat's ownership of an old Southern plantation.

> Harry Golden
> "A Day With Carl Sandburg"
> *Only in America*

Warrenton was my father's home. . . . that
architecturally distinguished town of about a
thousand people, once an important political and
social center of the state but becalmed after the Civil
War into the immemorial doze of small commerce,
tobacco and cotton marketing, and intense
reconnaissance of one's neighbors: the life of a
thousand other such towns.

Reynolds Price
"Home: An American Obsession"

Fig. 12. Eaton Place, Warrenton

Fig. 13. Eaton Place interior, Warrenton

Fig. 14. Nathaniel Green House, Warrenton

Fig. 15. Nathaniel Green House interior, Warrenton

Fig. 16. Somerville-Graham House, Warrenton

Fig. 17. Somerville-Graham House, Doric columns, Warrenton

Fig. 18. Somerville-Graham House, mantelpiece, Warrenton

When grate fires were lighted, or re-charged, early of a zingingly crisp fall morning, scented smoke came tumbling wildly as a covey of baby birds flying more from exuberance and liberation than from skill. When fires were prancing red ponies, the smoke was a black banner defying the demonic threats of the great white wolf of winter, who waited, almost ready to pounce upon Oxford, just above the horizon. A bit later on in the day the smoke smelled like good pipe tobacco.

Thad Stem, Jr.
Thad Stem's First Reader

Fig. 19. Edward Belo House, Winston-Salem

Fig. 20. Oakdale Cemetery, Hebrew gate, Wilmington

49

She would build them a . . . brick mansion, with Brussels carpets so soft they'd mire up to their knees when they walked on it, with electric lights, with fine furniture and a water closet. And she'd hire a cook and a butler to do all the work so they could sit on the porch — the front veranda — and talk polly-wogs all day. She might have to give Mama some fancy work to keep her hands still. And the cousins . . . some day she would pass them by in a rubber-tired carriage with her black coachman whipping two fine gray horses and silk tassels flying! . . .

Bernice Kelly Harris
Purslane

Fig. 21. Dr. Josephus Hall House, Salisbury

Fig. 22. The Barracks, Tarboro

Fig. 23. The Barracks, stairwell, Tarboro

Fig. 24. Bellamy Mansion, Wilmington

The Bellamy Mansion at 5th and Market Streets, which is considered to be a classic example of Greek Revival architecture, was built, excepting the columns, by free negro craftsmen. Work on the mansion began in 1857, at which time free negroes, for the most part, were employed for the masonry, carpentry and plaster work.

The beautiful Corinthian columns, with their exquisitely carved capitals, of which there were fourteen, were ordered to be made by a northern factory.

Lewis Philip Hall
Land of the Golden River

Fig. 25. Waldo-Darden Hotel, Hamilton

Fig. 26. Garland Buford House, Milton vicinity

Fig. 27. Garland Buford House, interior woodwork

Fig. 28. Cooleemee, Mocksville vicinity

. . . it was a mellow, delightful old place, in an excellent state of repair. It had a broad central hall, ample high-ceilinged rooms, long French windows, and hospitable verandas, the whole surrounded by towering trees in a wide grassy yard which gave the place privacy — even a degree of isolation.

John Harden
Tar Heel Ghosts

Fig. 29. Cooleemee, central stair, Mocksville vicinity

Fig. 30. Cooleemee, interior, Mocksville vicinity

Fig. 31. Inkwell House, Amity vicinity

Fig. 32. Blandwood, Greensboro

56

Fig. 33. Coolmore, Tarboro vicinity

Fig. 34. Caswell County Courthouse, Yanceyville

Fig. 35. Caswell County Courthouse, interior, Yanceyville

Fig. 36. Zebulon Latimer House, Wilmington

Fig. 37. Zebulon Latimer House, interior, Wilmington

. . . Wilmington to me is home. It is a very special place where the air is soft with salt moisture, the trees are hung with gray moss and ornamented with creamy magnolias . . . Wilmington is oyster roasts, swimming, sailing, bare feet, and long, slow walks down plaza-lined streets. In Wilmington I can hear the voices of my ancestors whispering in high-ceilinged rooms and on wind-swept sounds and beaches.

Anne Russell
Wilmington

Fig. 38. Griffin and Martin Law Office, Williamston

Fig. 39. Temple of Israel, Wilmington

Fig. 40. Temple of Israel, interior detail, Wilmington

Fig. 41. St. James Episcopal Church, Wilmington

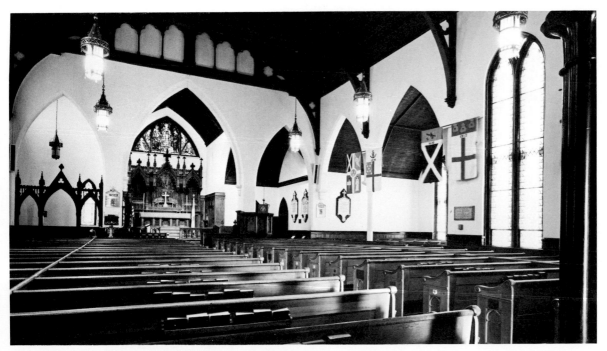

Fig. 42. St. James Episcopal Church, interior, Wilmington

Fig. 43. Christ Church (Episcopal), Raleigh

. . . a people and a tradition (are) symbolized only by tall Christ Church which remains unaltered since the time when the rooster on its weathervane was said to be the only poultry that was left in town after General Sherman's visit.

Jonathan Daniels
"Tarheel Capital"

Fig. 44. Christ Church, interior, Raleigh

Fig. 45. United Methodist Church, Fairfield

Fig. 46. United Methodist Church, interior, Fairfield

Fig. 47. St. Barnabas Episcopal Church, Snow Hill

Fig. 48. St. Barnabas Episcopal Church, interior, Snow Hill

Fig. 49. Commandant's House, Hillsborough

Fig. 50. Capehart House, Kittrell

Ryan stood on the sidewalk . . . looking up at the old curliqued house. It was exactly the same. . . . knobs and carvings hung from all the eaves and the roof of the porch. . . . Just for one minute the sight of the house wrung at his heart (he could not say why) and he thought of himself running in this house as a boy . . .

Doris Betts
Tall Houses in Winter

Fig. 51. Dr. A. B. Nobles House, Tarboro vicinity

Fig. 52. Cheshire-Nash House, Tarboro

Fig. 53. William Fields House, Greensboro

Fig. 57. Pippin House, interior, Tarboro

Fig. 58. Cabarrus County Courthouse, Concord

Fig. 59. Faith Hall, Barber-Scotia College, Concord

Fig. 60. Dodd-Hinsdale House, Raleigh

When she'd come here as a bride (the house) had
been full of heavy Victorian furniture and lamps
with stained glass shades. There were lace curtains
and velvet draperies at the windows that shut out
most of the light, and the tables were crowded with
gimcracks — vases, bowls, jugs, figurines, miniature
tea sets. Crocheted antimacassars on the chairs,
stuffed birds under bell-shaped glass domes, even
black marble statuary of nymphs and satyrs.

Mena Webb
The Curious Wine

Fig. 61. Redmond-Shackleford House, Tarboro

So, if this part of North Carolina is no longer a land of country sites, it has become a land of little towns. Some are raw and ugly under the Southern sun. But there are, too, old towns: the county seats of softness and charm, of wide shaded streets . . . of pleasant white houses with green blinds drawn, of old heavy trees without motion in August heat, of Confederate monuments on lonely watch now in unused parks, and of molding yellow courthouses with square clock towers and cupolas enveloped in the fluttering shadows of pigeons and sparrows.

Ovid Williams Pierce
"North Carolina"

Fig. 62. Redmond-Shackleford House, interior, Tarboro

There is a lightness, an airiness, a genteel whimsy about the late-Victorian dwelling. It is more than fantasy, more than a languid longing for a simpler age gone by that endows this late-Victorian house with its aura of charm. . . . Abundant windows . . . gave the home almost two dozen eyes to the world. . . . The eye dances up the tower, lingers on its hand-carved woodwork, and then easily imagines itself inside the cupola, secretly espying the world from behind lace curtains.

Sydney Nathans
The Quest for Progress

Fig. 63. Redmond-Shackleford House, interior, Tarboro

Fig. 64. Banker's House, Shelby

Fig. 65. John Milton Odell House, Concord

Fig. 66. Saluda Cottages, Flat Rock

Fig. 67. Saluda Cottages, interior, Flat Rock

Fig. 68. Saluda Cottages, interior, Flat Rock

Fig. 69. Heck House, Raleigh

Fig. 70. Mansard Roof House, Fayetteville

Below them lay the picturesque old town, a mass of vivid green, dotted here and there with gray roofs that rose above the tree-tops. . . . The market house and the slender spires of half a dozen churches were sharply outlined against the green background. . . . For many years before the rebellion a Federal arsenal had been located (there). . . . now only ruined walls and broken cannon remained of what had been the chief ornament and pride of Patesville. (Fayetteville)

Charles W. Chesnutt
The House Behind the Cedars

Fig. 71. Statesville City Hall

Fig. 72. Julius I. Foust Building, University of North Carolina at Greensboro

In May Cupid shoots blindfolded — millionaires marry stenographers, wise professors woo white-aproned gumchewers behind quick-lunch counters; schoolma'ams make big bad boys remain after school . . . old chaps put on white spats and promenade near the Normal School.

> O. Henry
> "The Marry Month of May"
> *Best Stories of O. Henry*

Fig. 73. All Souls' Episcopal Church, Biltmore Village, Asheville

Fig. 74. First Presbyterian Church Tower, Salisbury

Fig. 75. Biddle Hall, Johnson C. Smith University, Charlotte

Fig. 76. New Hanover County Courthouse, Wilmington

Fig. 77. North Carolina School for the Deaf, Morganton

Fig. 78. Belmont Abbey, Belmont

Fig. 79. United Methodist Church, tower detail, Oxford

Fig. 80. Chapel of St. Augustine's College, Raleigh

The Methodist bell wheezed, as if it has forgotten to take its flu shots, and the wind spun the steeple as if he had a string and it were a top. From the way the wind jumped up and down on the tops of the buildings, especially on those made of tin, you'd have thought old Goliath was daring everyone in town out to fight.

> Thad Stem, Jr.
> *Thad Stem's First Reader*

Fig. 81. St. Joseph's Episcopal Church, Fayetteville

Fig. 82. St. Joseph's Episcopal Church, interior, Fayetteville

Fig. 83. Executive Mansion, Raleigh

Once inside the city (the highway) goes sedately under the arched foliage of old trees before the multigabled gingerbread mansion of North Carolina's governor. Across the landscaped square are cupolaed mansions of the scroll-saw period of a South which some did not always find poor even after that war.

Jonathan Daniels
"Tarheel Capital"

Fig. 84. Executive Mansion, interior, Raleigh

Fig. 85. Col. Jacob Lott Ludlow House, Winston-Salem

Fig. 86. Col. Jacob Lott Ludlow House, interior, Winston-Salem

Fig. 87. Royster-Bryan House, Tarboro

Fig. 88. Royster-Bryan House, interior, Tarboro

Fig. 89. Hawkins-Hartness House, Raleigh

Fig. 90. Mott Simmons House, Statesville

Fig. 91. Mallonee-Jones House, Charlotte

Fig. 92. Liddell-McNinch House, Charlotte

At first glance the home of Jules Korner of
Kernersville . . . seems to deserve the name given to
it by contemporaries: Korner's Folly. Built in 1880,
the three-story, twenty-two-room residence spreads
every which way. A multiplicity of heights and levels
and a myriad of building materials give it the
appearance of a miniature castle, misbegotten in
stone, wood, and eight different sizes of handmade
brick. Its sharply pitched roof swarms with spirelike
chimneys; recessed arches and narrow windows
endlessly ornament the facade.

Sydney Nathans
The Quest for Progress

Fig. 93. Korner's Folly, Kernersville

Fig. 94. Korner's Folly, ballroom, Kernersville

Fig. 95. Victoria, Charlotte

If you had a lot of money you had a bay window on the front of the house nicely draped with red velvet with matching ball fringe. The bay window was usually complete with a table holding an ornate lamp, a potted fern, and/or sundry knick-knacks. And often, when my friends with bay windows (in their houses, of course) had parties, the punch bowl, cutglass and sparkling like diamonds, was often placed on the table in the window recess. To me, it seemed the epitome of luxury.

Zoe Kincaid Brockman
"Unguarded Moments"

Fig. 96. Victoria, interior, Charlotte

Fig. 97. Blades House, New Bern

Fig. 98. Blades House, interior, New Bern

Fig. 99. Charles T. Holt House, Haw River

The house looked real nice lit up, he thought, black floor and ceiling, that curly gray banister, the gray wicker furniture. Quincy had made sure that house was painted every other year, and paid the mortgage off besides.

Doris Betts
"The Glory of
His Nostrils"

Fig. 100. Charles T. Holt House, porch, Haw River

Fig. 101. Charles T. Holt House, gazebo, Haw River

Fig. 102. Capehart House, Raleigh

Fig. 103. Oakhurst, Oak Ridge

Fig. 104. Gaskill-Pierce House, Salisbury

102

It was a new home (and there were not many brand-new homes in Salisbury), papered very dark inside, as was the style, furnished with knobbed walnut furniture then in fashion, and with the few who had any money, just beginning to replace the inherited mahogany which most of us were keeping because we must. In the front parlour, our hostess had placed a gleaming punch bowl with decorative grapes and apples heaped about it. Several of the social set . . . stood about in decolletage, and served the guests. This formal dress was itself a daring innovation.

Hope Summerell Chamberlain
This Was Home

Fig. 105. L. H. Clement House, Salisbury

Fig. 106. James Dayvault House, Concord

Fig. 107. William G. Means House, Concord

The car moved . . . past the big, silent houses; old houses built of brick or wood clapboard, some with intricate curlicues of woodwork, a few with turrets and gables and upstairs porches. They sat far back on their lawns surrounded by shrubs and half hidden by trees. Everybody who was anybody lived in this neighborhood.

Mena Webb
The Curious Wine

Fig. 108. W. A. Thomas House, Statesville

Fig. 109. C. M. Steele House, Statesville

Fig. 110. Overcash House, Charlotte

Fig. 111. Daniel Branson Coltrane House, Concord

Her house was a good place to visit . . . a low porch
with twelve slender columns. There, in the summer,
in the shade of water oaks, Miss Effie, dressed in
black, would be sitting, knitting or embroidering,
while her big gray cat sat at, and sometimes on, her
feet. Slow, incertain music would be coming through
open windows from the music room . . .

Max Steele
"The Cat and the Coffee Drinkers"
Where She Brushed Her Hair and Other Stories

Fig. 112. J. P. Carr House, Charlotte

Fig. 113. Chatham County Courthouse, Pittsboro

Fig. 114. Broughton Hospital, Morganton

Fig. 115. Thomas Wolfe Memorial, Asheville

In Asheville, it isn't necessary any longer to search for the path of Thomas Wolfe. The same public libraries which wouldn't have *Look Homeward, Angel* upon their shelves now have his picture on their walls. A historical marker rises near the busy traffic of Pack Square to point toward his old residence a block or two away. "Dixieland," once a boardinghouse run by his mother, is now a shrine.

Ovid Williams Pierce
"North Carolina"

110

Fig. 116. Rumbough House, Asheville

Fig. 117. Biltmore House, Asheville

My house is rather a heavy set cottage and is made from the trees which grew where the house now stands. . . . George Vanderbilt's extensive new grounds command a fine view of my place. . . . One can see from the foundations of his prospective mansion for miles up the beautiful French Broad River, and the smoky tops of the soft, blue mountains make a magnificent picture of gentleness and repose.

. . . One reason I have not yet finished my place is that I want first to see what George does, and thus get the advantage of his experience. He does not mind that he says.

Bill Nye
"Rural Retreat"

Fig. 118. Biltmore House, staircase, Asheville

Fig. 119. Biltmore House, library, Asheville

Fig. 120. Biltmore House, Palm Court, Asheville

Fig. 121. Columbia Manufacturing Company, Ramseur

And so the cotton mill village has long been an important feature in the physical and social landscape of the South. The main outlines of the pattern were set before the Civil War by pioneering mills such as . . . Spray and Alamance, North Carolina, and many others: a few houses, a little school, a little church, a handful of families, and an owner-manager . . . who took a fatherly interest in his people, protected them from the evils of drink by prohibiting saloons, eliminated "undesirables" from the community, helped the needy.

Harriet L. Herring
Passing of the Mill Village

Fig. 122. Glencoe Mill Village, company store

The company-owned mill village, offering the workers benefits but also tying their lives to the company, has all but vanished. The homes have been sold to their occupants, or to others, or have been torn down. The mill owners have found that it is difficult enough to be efficient manufacturers without the additional burdens of operating a real estate business and supervising the living conditions of their workers.

Broadus Mitchell
The Rise of the Cotton Mill Village in the South

Fig. 123. Glencoe Mill Village

Fig. 124. Coleridge Mill Village housing

Fig. 125. Coleridge Mill Village housing

. . . tobacco stemmeries rising flush from the sidewalks — outmoded structures these, with flat facades of smoke-darkened red brick and, along their roof lines, a graduated edge of ornamental turreting which gives them the serene and incongruous look of Italian palaces . . .

I inhaled the odor of the bright leaf (the odor of home) which is richest in early fall, and I felt that in the confusion of this hodge-podge city, which has not yet decided what it really is or wishes to become, was the raw juicy stuff of life itself. And what is more charming than that?

Frances Gray Patton
"The Town Bull
Durham Built"

Fig. 126. Bull Durham Tobacco Company, Durham

Fig. 127. Tobacco Warehouse, Durham

Fig. 128. Duke Homestead, Durham

I have excellent hubris. I am a historic house. I am
the first house ever built in this town. I existed
before the Civil War and I never was a mansion. I am
the poor house of a poor dirt farmer of the
Piedmont . . .

Daphne Athas
Entering Ephesus

Fig. 129. Pomona Terra Cotta Manufacturing Company, Greensboro

Fig. 130. Zollicoffer's Law Office, Henderson

Fig. 131. Gidden's Jewelry, Goldsboro

Fig. 132. Gidden's Jewelry, interior, Goldsboro

Fig. 133. Merchants and Farmers National Bank Building, Charlotte

Fig. 134. McMullen Building, Elizabeth City

The Blue Light scorns the labor-saving arts of modern pharmacy. It macerates its opium and percolates its own laudanum and paregoric. To this day pills are made behind its tall prescription desk. . . . The store is on a corner about which coveys of ragged-plumed, hilarious children play and become candidates for the cough drops and soothing syrups that wait for them inside.

> O. Henry
> "The Love-Philtre of
> Ikey Schoenstein"
> *Best Stories of O. Henry*

Fig. 135. Fordham Drug Store, Greensboro

Fig. 136. Fordham Drug Store, interior, Greensboro

Fig. 137. Will Waldrop House and General Store, Sandy Mush

Fig. 138. Payne's Chapel, Sandy Mush

Fig. 139. Seaboard-Coastline Railroad Station, Hamlet

The depot, itself, if not a thing of beauty, was close to a joy forever. It was a hub, a magnet, a focal point. It was a poor man's country club, a forum, a debating society, and all of this was put to the eerie arabesques of the telegraph key that had a million flying fingers and a million singing tongues. The operator was a man of mystery and awe. His thumping instrument was a bottomless geyser of fact and wisdom. Into his cunning ears poured the history the land made each hour and the fabulous news from the far marts of creation.

Thad Stem, Jr.
Thad Stem's First Reader

Fig. 140. Railroad House, Sanford

Fig. 141. Railroad House, detail, Sanford

Fig. 142. Glendale Springs Hotel

Halfway up the mountains, on the verandas of the hotels, 19th Century white-frame buildings, all windows, row above row, rising out of rhododendron and laurel, the elderly are sitting in the circles of rockers — gray-haired ladies and a few gentlemen, wearing light coats against the chill. They have come up to spend the hot months, as they have been doing for twenty-five years, to this same porch, wrapped in afternoon mist, to remember those once here, to whom the circle of chairs earlier belonged. . . .

     Ovid Williams Pierce
     "North Carolina"

Fig. 143. Carolina Hotel, Pinehurst

Fig. 144. Currituck Beach Lighthouse, Currituck

Maybe lighthouses are no longer needed. But if the time comes when the century-old towers at Cape Hatteras and Cape Lookout, and at Bodie Island and Currituck Beach are abandoned; and if the even older structures at Bald Head and Ocracoke are declared surplus, it will mark the end of a glorious period of history on the North Carolina coast.

David Stick
North Carolina Lighthouses

Fig. 145. Cape Hatteras Lighthouse